CHRISTMAS AT HOME

WITH

Mary & Martha

Cookin' Up Traditional Dishes & Faith

BARBOUR
PUBLISHING

© 2006 by Barbour Publishing, Inc.

ISBN 1-59789-433-8

All rights reserved. No part of this publication may be reproduced or transmitted for commercial purposes, except for brief quotations in printed reviews, without written permission of the publisher.

Churches and other noncommercial interests may reproduce portions of this book without the express written permission of Barbour Publishing, provided that the text does not exceed 500 words or 5 percent of the entire book, whichever is less, and that the text is not material quoted from another publisher. When reproducing text from this book, include the following credit line: "From *Christmas at Home with Mary & Martha: Cookin' Up Traditional Dishes and Faith*, published by Barbour Publishing, Inc. Used by permission."

Recipes were compiled from the following titles, all published by Barbour Publishing, Inc.: *Heart's Delight*, *Homemade Christmas Cookies*, *Holiday Desserts*, *Holiday Jar Mixes*, *No-Bake Holiday Recipes*, *Traditional Christmas Favorites*, *101 Christmas Recipe Ideas*, *Holiday Snacks and Appetizers*, and *Homemade Christmas Sweets*.

All scripture quotations are taken from the HOLY BIBLE, NEW INTERNATIONAL VERSION®. NIV®. Copyright © 1973, 1978, 1984 by International Bible Society. Used by permission of Zondervan. All rights reserved.

Cover Design by Greg Jackson, Thinkpen Design, LLC.
Cover and Interior artwork by Karen M. Reilly

Published by Barbour Publishing, Inc., P.O. Box 719, Uhrichsville, Ohio 44683, www.barbourbooks.com

Our mission is to publish and distribute inspirational products offering exceptional value and biblical encouragement to the masses.

ECPA Member of the Evangelical Christian Publishers Association

Printed in Canada.
5 4 3 2 1

CONTENTS

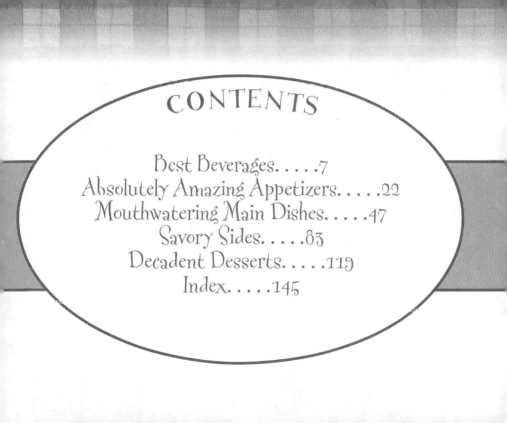

Time was with most of us, when Christmas Day, encircling all our limited world like a magic ring, left nothing out for us to miss or seek: bound together all our home enjoyments, affections, and hopes; grouped everything and everyone round the Christmas fire, and made the little picture shining in our bright young eyes complete.
CHARLES DICKENS

Meet Mary & Martha. . .

If you love celebrating Christmas with a big family feast, then this holiday cookbook is just for you. Featuring everything from the best beverages to mouthwatering main dishes and decadent desserts—if it'll top off your seasonal celebration, it's in here! We'll be appearing throughout the book, offering you tips and inspiration to make your Christmas just a bit merrier—*and* more meaningful. Ready to cook up some traditional dishes and faith this season? Roll up your sleeves, put on that apron, and. . . Happy cooking!

With love (from our kitchen to yours),
Mary & Martha

Best Beverages

Faith is the root of all blessings.
JEREMY TAYLOR

Christmas Punch

1 quart grape juice
1 pint lemon juice
1 bottle carbonated water
1 pint ginger ale or sweet juice
1 pint orange juice
½ pint pineapple juice

Mix all ingredients and pour into punch bowl with block of ice.
Pineapple or orange slices may be used as garnish.
Makes about 2 gallons of punch.

To dress up your punch bowl, float slices of orange and pineapple on top. If desired, add maraschino cherries.

Creamy Dreamy Hot Chocolate

1 (14 ounce) can sweetened condensed milk
½ cup unsweetened cocoa powder
2 teaspoons vanilla
⅛ teaspoon salt
6½ cups hot water

Combine first four ingredients in large saucepan; mix well. Over medium heat, slowly stir in water. Cook until heated through, stirring frequently.

Eggnog

4 eggs, separated
½ cup sugar, divided
2 cups cold milk
1 cup cold light cream
1½ teaspoons vanilla
⅛ teaspoon salt
¼ teaspoon ground nutmeg

Beat egg yolks together with ¼ cup sugar until thick. Gradually mix in milk, cream, vanilla, salt, and nutmeg, beating until frothy. Beat egg whites with remaining sugar until mixture forms soft peaks; then fold into egg yolk mixture. Cover and chill. Mix well before serving and sprinkle with nutmeg.

Step out in faith and trust God to provide for all your needs this Christmas. If your needs seem too great, remember that the Lord likes to surprise us in big ways. Talk to God; He's listening.

Fresh Berry Punch

1 (12 ounce) bag fresh cranberries
3 cups water
1 envelope raspberry drink mix
1 can frozen pineapple juice concentrate, thawed
1 large banana, mashed
1 (2 liter) bottle ginger ale

Puree 2 cups cranberries. Combine pureed cranberries, remaining whole cranberries, and water in large saucepan. Cook over high heat until cranberries begin to pop; remove from heat. Stir in remaining ingredients except ginger ale. Freeze about 12 hours, stir, and refreeze.

TO SERVE:
Puree slush in food processor, spoon into pitcher,
and mix in ginger ale.

Fruit Slush

1 medium can frozen orange juice concentrate, thawed
½ cup lemon juice
2 cans crushed pineapple, with juice
3 cups water
2 cups sugar
3 to 4 diced bananas
1 (10 ounce) jar maraschino cherries

Mix together and put in freezer until slushy, or freeze
and take out and thaw until slushy.

Hot Cappuccino

1 cup instant hot chocolate mix
½ cup instant coffee granules (good quality)
½ cup powdered nondairy coffee creamer
½ cup powdered skim milk
1¼ teaspoons ground cinnamon
¼ teaspoon ground nutmeg
Boiling water
Chocolate, grated (optional)

Mix dry ingredients well. Use ¼ cup mixture for each 2 cups boiling water.
Blend desired amount until foamy and pour into mugs.
Sprinkle with grated chocolate if desired.

When the family is sitting down for the annual viewing of It's a Wonderful Life, *prepare a tubful of popcorn to go with a hot drink. Dress up the popcorn with a shake of spices, a drizzle of melted chocolate, or a sprinkle of cheese.*

Perky Punch

1 small can orange juice concentrate, thawed
1 small can lemonade concentrate, thawed
1 envelope strawberry Kool-Aid (unsweetened)
1 envelope cherry Kool-Aid (unsweetened)
1 tall can tropical fruit punch
2 (12 ounce) bottles ginger ale

Prepare orange juice and lemonade according to directions on cans.
Add Kool-Aid using half amount of water and 2 cups sugar required.
Add tropical fruit punch. Pour into punch bowl; add ginger ale and ice cubes.

Sparkling Cranberry Punch

2 quarts cranberry juice cocktail, chilled
1 (6 ounce) can frozen lemonade concentrate, thawed
1 quart sparkling water, chilled

Mix cranberry juice cocktail and lemonade concentrate in large punch bowl.
Just before serving, stir in chilled sparkling water. Makes twenty-five ½-cup servings.

Spiced Tea

4 tea bags orange pekoe tea
Juice of 3 oranges and 3 lemons
4 teaspoons ground cinnamon
1½ teaspoons ground cloves
2 cups sugar
16 cups (1 gallon) water

Combine all ingredients in large saucepan.
Simmer for 20 minutes then remove tea bags. Serve.

Wassail

2 quarts apple juice
2 cups orange juice
1 cup lemon juice
1 (18 ounce) can pineapple juice
1 stick cinnamon
1 teaspoon ground cloves
½ cup sugar

Combine all ingredients in large saucepan. Bring to a boil. Reduce
heat and simmer, uncovered, for 1 hour. Serve warm.

Create a holiday atmosphere with aroma. Have a Crock-Pot of wassail simmering in the room before your guests arrive. Add orange slices to float on the top, and let the heated spices fill the room with a homey fragrance.

Absolutely Amazing Appetizers

Faith expects from God what is beyond all expectation.
ANDREW MURRAY

Baked Water Chestnuts

1 can whole water chestnuts
½ cup soy sauce
Sugar
4 slices bacon, cut in half lengthwise and widthwise

Drain water chestnuts. Marinate in soy sauce for 30 minutes. Drain sauce from water chestnuts and roll each water chestnut in sugar. Wrap each chestnut in strip of bacon. Bake at 400° for 30 minutes.

Chicken Bites

4 boneless, skinless chicken breasts
1 cup finely crushed round butter crackers (about 24)
½ cup Parmesan cheese, grated
¼ cup walnuts, finely chopped
1 teaspoon dried thyme leaves
1 teaspoon dried basil leaves
½ teaspoon seasoned salt
¼ teaspoon black pepper
½ cup margarine or butter, melted

Place aluminum foil over 2 baking sheets. Cut chicken into 1-inch pieces. Combine cracker crumbs, Parmesan cheese, walnuts, thyme, basil, seasoned salt, and pepper. Heat oven to 400°. Dip chicken pieces into melted margarine, then into crumb mixture. Place chicken pieces on cookie sheets and bake, uncovered, for 20 to 25 minutes or until golden brown. Makes about 6 dozen appetizers.

Christmas Cheese Ball

1 (8 ounce) package cream cheese, softened
2 cups cheddar cheese, shredded
2 green onions, chopped
1 (2 ounce) jar diced pimientos, drained
2 teaspoons Worcestershire sauce
1 teaspoon lemon juice

In mixing bowl, beat together all ingredients until smooth. Spoon mixture into small bowl lined with plastic wrap. Chill until firm. When ready to serve, invert onto serving plate. Serve with crackers.

Give a gift that keeps on giving. Buy a very smooth, very nice piece of maple wood—a 1-inch thick board 8 to 10 inches wide. Cut it so that you have a square. Sand the rough edges. Seal with a quality sealant. Give the cheese board with your best cheese ball and a cheese knife or spreader.

Cocktail Meatballs

MEATBALLS:
1 pound ground beef
1 egg
½ cup bread crumbs
½ cup ketchup
1 tablespoon parsley flakes
½ teaspoon onion powder
½ teaspoon seasoned salt
1 pinch black pepper

SAUCE:
1 (14 ounce) bottle hot or regular ketchup
2 tablespoons cornstarch
1 (12 ounce) jar apple jelly
1 (12 ounce) jar currant jelly

Combine meatball ingredients. Mix well and shape into 1-inch balls. Place on rack in shallow pan. Bake at 350° for 10 to 15 minutes. Combine ketchup and cornstarch. Stir in jellies. Spoon on top of meatballs and serve.

Crab-Stuffed Mushrooms

1 (6 ounce) tin crabmeat
1 egg, well beaten
¼ cup fine bread crumbs
¼ cup tomato juice
1 teaspoon lemon juice
1 dash Tabasco
1 teaspoon onion, finely chopped
2 teaspoons celery, finely chopped
½ teaspoon salt
1 pound mushrooms
½ cup fine bread crumbs
¼ cup butter or margarine, melted

Mix first nine ingredients and fill mushroom caps. Toss remaining bread crumbs with melted butter and sprinkle over filled caps. Brown 6 inches from heat for 5 to 8 minutes, or bake at 350° for 15 to 20 minutes.

Easy Onion Chip Dip

1 package onion soup mix
1 (16 ounce) container sour cream

Mix well; serve with plain or rippled chips.

Great Christmas gifts for the culinarily inclined include measuring spoons and cups, spices, apron, kitchen timer, recipe box, cookbook, small mixing bowls, whisk... Visit your local supermarket for other fun gift ideas.

Easy Taco Dip

1 (8 ounce) package cream cheese, softened
1 cup sour cream
1 package taco seasoning, or to taste
1 cup iceburg lettuce, chopped
1 cup tomatoes, chopped and drained
Green onions, chopped
Cheddar cheese, shredded

Combine first three ingredients and spread in shallow round dish.
Layer with iceberg lettuce and tomatoes. Top with chopped green onions and shredded cheddar cheese. Serve with tortilla chips.

Guacamole Bites

2 tubes refrigerated crescent rolls
½ teaspoon cumin
½ teaspoon chili powder
1 (8 ounce) package cream cheese, softened
1 container (1½ cups) guacamole or 3 mashed ripe avocados
1 tomato, chopped
¼ cup bacon bits
¼ cup sliced ripe black olives

Separate crescent rolls into long rectangles, place on ungreased cookie sheet, and press over bottom of sheet. Sprinkle with cumin and chili powder, and bake at 375° for 17 minutes or until golden brown. Cool. Combine cream cheese and guacamole until smooth, spread over crust, and chill. Top with remaining ingredients. Makes 60 appetizers.

Honey-Glazed Chicken Wings

3 pounds chicken wings
⅓ cup soy sauce
2 tablespoons vegetable oil
2 tablespoons chili sauce (or ketchup or barbecue sauce)
¼ cup honey
1 teaspoon salt
½ teaspoon ground ginger
¼ teaspoon garlic powder (or 1 clove garlic, minced)
¼ teaspoon cayenne pepper

Separate wings at joints. Mix remaining ingredients. Pour over chicken. Cover and refrigerate, turning chicken occasionally, at least one hour or overnight. Heat oven to 375°. Drain chicken, reserving marinade. Place chicken on rack in foil-lined broiler pan. Bake for 30 minutes. Brush chicken with reserved marinade. Turn chicken and bake for another 30 minutes or until tender.

Hot Artichoke and Spinach Dip

½ cup sour cream
½ cup mayonnaise
½ cup Parmesan cheese, grated
½ cup mozzarella cheese, shredded
1 to 2 teaspoons minced garlic
1 package frozen spinach, thawed and well drained
1 (14 ounce) can artichoke hearts

Combine all ingredients. Place in shallow casserole dish.
Bake at 325° for 15 to 20 minutes or until bubbly.

Hot Ryes

1 cup Swiss cheese, finely shredded
¼ cup cooked, crumbled bacon
1 (4½ ounce) can chopped ripe black olives
¼ cup minced onion
1 teaspoon Worcestershire sauce
¼ cup mayonnaise
1 loaf party rye bread

Mix first six ingredients together. Spread 2 to 3 teaspoons of mixture on slices of bread. Bake at 375° for 10 to 15 minutes or until bubbly.

Magic Meatball Sauce

1 can cream of chicken soup
1 (1 pound 10 ounce) jar traditional spaghetti sauce
1 (18 ounce) bottle spicy honey barbecue sauce

Melt soup in microwave. (It is almost solid and will cause your sauce to be lumpy if you don't melt it first.) Place all ingredients in Crock-Pot and add cooked, defrosted meatballs. Simmer until heated through.

Mini Meat Pies

36 mini tart shells, baked

FILLING:
1 medium onion, chopped
2 tablespoons butter
1 pound ground veal or beef
1 pound ground pork
1 can cream of mushroom soup
Salt, black pepper, and garlic to taste

Sauté onions in butter; add meat and cook until browned. Add soup and spices.
Cool filling before adding to tart shells. Serve.

Nuts and Bolts

4 to 5 tablespoons butter or margarine
2 teaspoons Worcestershire sauce
1½ teaspoons onion powder
1½ teaspoons garlic or seasoned salt
2 cups toasted oats cereal
2 cups corn squares cereal
2 cups wheat squares cereal
2 cups pretzels

Melt butter or margarine. Add Worcestershire sauce and spices. Combine all other ingredients in large microwave-safe dish. Add melted mixture and stir well. Microwave on high for 4 to 5 minutes, stirring twice. Cool.

Pita Bites

1 bag pitas, halved and cut into triangles, or mini pitas
1 cup mayonnaise
1 onion, chopped
½ cup slivered almonds
½ pound cheddar cheese, shredded
6 slices cooked, crumbled bacon

Combine all ingredients except pitas. Spread mixture on top of pitas.
Bake at 400° for 8 to 10 minutes.

Sausage Cheese Balls

1½ cups all-purpose baking mix
4 cups (16 ounces) sharp cheddar cheese, shredded
2 pounds ground pork sausage
½ cup onion, finely chopped
½ cup celery, finely chopped
½ teaspoon garlic powder

Mix all ingredients and roll into 1-inch balls. Bake at 375° for 15 minutes on ungreased cookie sheet, until golden brown. Makes about 6 dozen appetizers.

During the Advent season, create a "prayer card" jar. As you receive Christmas cards in the mail, add them to the jar. At suppertime each evening, pull one card from the jar and say a special prayer for the sender.

Let us not love with words or tongue but with actions and in truth.
1 JOHN 3:18

Shrimp Spread

2 (8 ounce) packages cream cheese, softened
½ cup mayonnaise
½ cup lemon juice
2 (4.5 ounce) cans cocktail shrimp, rinsed, drained, and chopped
1 tablespoon prepared horseradish
1 to 2 tablespoons green onion, finely chopped
⅛ teaspoon garlic salt

In mixing bowl, beat cream cheese until fluffy. Beat in mayonnaise and lemon juice. Stir in shrimp, then add remaining ingredients. Refrigerate to blend flavors, then serve with crackers or vegetables.

Stuffed Tomato Bites

2 pints cherry tomatoes
1 (8 ounce) package cream cheese, softened
6 slices cooked, crumbled bacon
2 green onions, minced
1 teaspoon parsley flakes

Slice off a thin layer from the top of each tomato. Scoop out pulp and discard it. Drain tomatoes well. In small bowl, beat together cream cheese, crumbled bacon, onions, and parsley. Spoon or pipe into tomato shells. Chill.

For a quick sweet appetizer, split open whole dates and stuff a large piece of walnut in each. Coat the dates in white granulated sugar and serve to your guests as they wait for the main course.

Sour-Sweet Wiener Tidbits

¾ cup prepared mustard
1 cup currant jelly
1 pound bite-sized wieners or cocktail sausages

Combine mustard and jelly in top of double boiler, then heat.
Add bite-sized wieners; heat thoroughly.

Teriyaki Meatballs

2 eggs
2 pounds ground round steak
½ cup cornflake crumbs
½ cup milk

2 tablespoons onion, grated
1 teaspoon salt
¼ teaspoon black pepper

Mix all ingredients and form into meatballs, about 1½ inches in diameter.
Bake at 300° for 45 minutes, turning and braising every 15 minutes.

SAUCE:

1 cup soy sauce
2 teaspoons ginger juice or
   1 teaspoon ground ginger

½ cup water
2 cloves garlic, minced
1 teaspoon sugar

Combine all sauce ingredients and spoon over meatballs, cooking until heated through.

Mouthwatering Main Dishes

Faith brings man to God;
love brings Him to man.
MARTIN LUTHER

Asparagus Ham Quiche

1 (10 ounce) package frozen cut asparagus
½ pound cooked ham, chopped
1 cup cheddar cheese, shredded
¼ cup onion, chopped
3 eggs
1 cup milk
¾ cup all-purpose baking mix
¼ teaspoon black pepper

In greased 9-inch pie pan, layer asparagus, ham, cheese, and onion.
Beat eggs and milk in small mixing bowl. Add baking mix and pepper.
Pour into pie pan. Bake at 375°for 30 minutes or until done.

You take time to dress up your holiday table, but don't forget your chairs. To keep the holiday spirit going, tie an evergreen or holly spray to the back of each chair and top it with a bow.

Baked Spaghetti

1 (8 ounce) box spaghetti, cooked and drained
1 pound hamburger, browned and drained
1 cup mozzarella cheese, shredded
1 jar spaghetti sauce

Mix together spaghetti, hamburger, and cheese. Add sauce. Spray casserole dish with cooking spray. Put mixture in dish and cover with additional shredded cheese if desired. Bake at 250° for 35 to 40 minutes.

Buttermilk Baked Cod

1½ pounds cod fillets
½ cup butter, melted
1 teaspoon salt
1 teaspoon paprika
1 teaspoon garlic powder
1 teaspoon lemon juice
1 cup buttermilk
2 cups herb-seasoned stuffing mix

Rinse and dry cod fillets; cut into serving pieces. Melt butter; add salt, paprika, garlic powder, and lemon juice. Dip fish in buttermilk; roll in stuffing. Place in foil-lined 9 x 13-inch baking pan. Drizzle butter mixture over fish. Bake at 450° for 10 to 15 minutes.

Candied Pork Chops

4 to 6 pork chops
2 to 3 apples, sliced with cores removed
Brown sugar
½ cup butter or margarine

Brown pork chops on both sides in skillet in small amount of oil. Heat oven to 350°. Line bottom of 9 x 13-inch pan with apple slices. Sprinkle apple slices generously with brown sugar. Dot with thin pats of butter or margarine. Place browned pork chops on top.
Bake at 350° for 1 hour, turning chops halfway through.
Baste chops often with juice from apples and brown sugar.

Invite a lonely neighbor to your Christmas Eve church service. After the service, stop for coffee and dessert, and share how the Lord has changed your life.

Cavatini

1 pound ground beef
⅛ teaspoon garlic powder
1 onion, chopped
1 green pepper, chopped
1 package sliced pepperoni
1 small can mushrooms, drained
32 ounces spaghetti sauce
½ pound curly noodles, cooked and drained
½ pound mozzarella cheese, shredded

Brown ground beef; add garlic powder, onion, and green pepper. Cook until tender, then drain. Stir in pepperoni, mushrooms, and spaghetti sauce. Grease 9 x 13-inch pan. Layer cooked noodles and cheese. Add ground beef mixture. Top with additional cheese. Bake at 375° for 35 to 40 minutes. Let stand for 5 to 10 minutes before serving.

Chicken Sausage Stuffing

4 tablespoons vegetable oil, divided
1 pound chicken or turkey sausage,
  removed from casing
1 large onion, chopped
2 celery ribs, chopped
2 large eggs
3 cups cubed stale pumpernickel bread

1 (10 to 12 pound) turkey, thawed if frozen
1 teaspoon sage
1 teaspoon paprika
½ teaspoon salt
¼ teaspoon black pepper
2 cups chicken broth

Heat 2 tablespoons oil in large skillet over medium heat. Add sausage and cook for
5 to 7 minutes or until lightly browned. Turn into large bowl and set aside. Heat
remaining 2 tablespoons oil in same frying pan and add onion and celery, cooking for
3 to 5 minutes or until tender. Add to bowl with sausage and cool. Mix eggs and bread
well. Preheat oven to 350°. Remove neck and giblets from turkey and rinse turkey
inside and out. Pat dry and season turkey with sage, paprika, salt, and pepper. Stuff
loosely with filling. Place turkey in large roasting pan with breast side up. Pour
chicken broth around turkey and roast for 3½ to 4 hours or until bird is tender
and juices run clear when thigh is pricked with a fork. Baste every 30 minutes.

Cider Baked Ham

1 (6 to 8 pound) bone-in ham
Whole cloves
3 cups apple cider

Place ham on rack in roasting pan; score ham in diamond pattern with sharp knife. Stud ham with whole cloves. Pour apple cider over ham. Bake at 325° for 20 minutes per pound of meat until meat thermometer inserted in ham reads 160°, basting every half hour with cider. Let ham stand for at least 5 minutes before carving.

Country Pork 'n' Kraut

2 pounds country-style pork ribs
1 medium onion, chopped
1 tablespoon vegetable oil
1 (14 ounce) can sauerkraut, undrained
1 cup applesauce
1 teaspoon garlic powder
2 tablespoons brown sugar

Cook ribs and onion in oil until ribs are browned and onion is tender. Place in Crock-Pot. Combine remaining ingredients and pour over ribs. Cook on high for 4 to 6 hours or until ribs are tender. May also be cooked in Dutch oven and baked at 350° for 1½ to 2 hours.

Cranberry Chicken

6 boneless, skinless chicken breast halves
1 can whole-berry cranberry sauce
1 large Granny Smith apple, peeled and diced
½ cup raisins
1 teaspoon orange peel
¼ cup walnuts, chopped
1 teaspoon curry powder
1 teaspoon ground cinnamon

Place chicken in greased 9 x 13-inch baking dish. Bake at 350° for 20 minutes. While chicken is cooking, combine remaining ingredients. Spoon cranberry mixture over chicken. Return to oven for 20 to 25 minutes or until chicken juices run clear.

Cranberry Pork Roast

1 lean, boneless pork roast (size can vary)
1 can jellied cranberry sauce
½ cup cranberry juice
½ cup sugar
1 teaspoon dry mustard
⅛ teaspoon ground cloves

Place roast in Crock-Pot. Combine remaining ingredients and pour over roast.
Cook on low for 6 to 8 hours. Thicken juice with cornstarch.
Makes terrific gravy for mashed potatoes.

Creamy Baked Chicken Breasts

4 boneless, skinless chicken breasts
4 slices Swiss cheese
1 can cream of chicken soup (thin with water to pour)
2 cups herb-seasoned stuffing mix
½ cup butter, melted (optional)

Place chicken in baking dish. Add cheese slice on top of each. Pour soup over all. Sprinkle with stuffing mix. Drizzle butter on top. Bake, uncovered, at 350°for 50 to 55 minutes.

Crescent Roll Chicken

3 boneless, skinless chicken breasts, cooked and cut into small pieces
1 can cream of chicken soup
½ cup cheddar cheese, shredded (optional)
½ cup milk
1 tube refrigerated crescent rolls

Combine soup, cheese, and milk. Pour half in 9 x 13-inch pan. Separate rolls;
place as much cut-up chicken in each roll as will fit; roll up, tucking in edges.
Place in pan. Spoon other half of sauce over rolls. Sprinkle shredded cheese over
all (optional). Bake at 350° for 25 to 30 minutes or until lightly browned.

Note: If using 29-ounce can of chicken soup,
use more cheese and 2 packages of crescent rolls.

Deluxe Roast Beef

3 or more pounds roast beef (rump roast, bottom round, or eye of round)
1 to 2 onions, sliced
1 can cream of celery soup
1 can cream of mushroom soup
½ soup can of water

Line 9 x 13-inch baking dish with plenty of foil to cover and seal the meat.
Heat oven to 325°. Trim excess fat from meat if desired. Place meat in center of foil-lined
pan. Place onion slices on top and sides of meat. In medium-sized bowl, combine soups.
Add water. Stir soup mixture well. Spoon over beef, moistening all visible meat.
Seal in aluminum foil. Cook at 325° for about 45 minutes a pound.

Family Delight Ham Loaf

2 or more pounds ground ham, according to taste
½ to 1 pound lean ground chuck
1 to 1½ cups bread crumbs
2 eggs, unbeaten
½ to 1 cup brown sugar
1 (15 to 16 ounce) can crushed pineapple, with juice
1 to 2 tablespoons mustard

Mix all ingredients together and press into glass or metal oblong baking dish.
Bake at 350° for 45 minutes to 1 hour. Cut into cubes.
For a festive holiday treat, put a maraschino or candied cherry half on top of each cube.

Festive Fajitas

3 to 4 boneless, skinless chicken breasts
1 tablespoon vegetable oil
¼ teaspoon garlic powder
1 cup green pepper, cut into strips
¾ cup onion, sliced
1 (10 ounce) package Mexican-style processed cheese
1 package 8-inch tortillas
1 cup tomato, chopped

Slice chicken breasts into thin strips and stir-fry in oil and garlic powder until no longer pink. Add green pepper strips and onion slices. Continue to stir-fry for 5 minutes. Cut cheese into cubes and add to chicken. Stir until cheese is melted; do not allow to boil. Place desired amount of chicken-cheese mixture in center of each tortilla. Top with chopped tomatoes. Fold.

Fettuccini Alfredo

6 ounces fettuccini, uncooked
¼ cup butter or margarine
¾ cup Parmesan cheese, grated
½ cup heavy whipping cream
2 tablespoons fresh parsley, chopped (optional)

Cook fettuccini according to package directions; drain. Meanwhile, in small saucepan, melt butter over medium heat; gradually stir in cheese, then add whipping cream, stirring until well blended. Continue heating sauce, stirring constantly, just to boiling point. Remove from heat; stir in parsley. Pour over noodles.
Can also add chicken, shrimp, bacon bits, or whatever you like.

Garlic Prime Rib

1 (10 pound) prime rib roast
Salt and black pepper to taste
5 cloves garlic, minced
½ cup Dijon mustard

Score roast. Season with salt and pepper. In small bowl, combine garlic and mustard.
Spread garlic mixture over roast. Place roast in roasting pan and cover. Roast at 500°
for 1 hour, then turn off oven. Leave oven door closed for 90 minutes, then test internal
temperature of roast. For a medium-rare roast, the temperature should be at least 140°; for
a medium roast, the temperature should be 155°.

Herbed Cornish Hens

3 frozen Rock Cornish hens (about 1 pound each), thawed
Salt and black pepper to taste
¼ cup margarine or butter, melted
½ teaspoon dried marjoram leaves
½ teaspoon dried thyme leaves
¼ teaspoon paprika
Watercress

Rub salt and pepper into cavities of hens. Place hens in shallow baking pan, breast side up. Combine margarine, marjoram, thyme, and paprika; brush portion of mixture on hens. Roast uncovered at 350°, brushing with remaining margarine mixture 5 or 6 times until done (about 1 hour). Cut each hen into halves with scissors, cutting along backbone from tail to neck and down center of breast. Garnish with watercress.

Lasagna

1 pound Italian sausage
1 clove garlic, minced
1 tablespoon whole basil
1½ teaspoons salt
1 (14.5 ounce) can tomatoes
2 (6 ounce) cans tomato paste
10 ounces lasagna noodles

2 eggs
3 cups fresh ricotta or cream-style
    cottage cheese
2 tablespoons parsley flakes
1 teaspoon salt
½ teaspoon black pepper
1 pound mozzarella cheese,
    thinly sliced

Brown sausage slowly and spoon off excess fat. Add next five ingredients plus 1 cup water and simmer, covered, for 15 minutes; stir frequently. Cook noodles in boiling salt water until tender. Beat eggs and add remaining ingredients except mozzarella. Layer half the lasagna noodles in 9 x 13 x 2-inch baking dish; spread with half of ricotta filling, then half of mozzarella cheese and half of meat sauce. Repeat. Bake at 375° for 30 minutes. Serves 8 to 10.

Lemon-Pepper Chicken

5 boneless, skinless chicken breasts
½ cup margarine
Lemon-pepper seasoning
1 can cream of mushroom soup
Cooked rice

Melt margarine in large skillet over medium heat. Add chicken breasts to skillet; sprinkle liberally with lemon-pepper seasoning. Cover with lid and let cook about 5 minutes. Turn breasts over and sprinkle with seasoning again. Turn breasts over again, in 5 to 7 minutes, to keep from burning. Cook approximately 20 to 25 minutes, if frozen. When chicken is done, remove from skillet. Stir canned soup into butter and drippings left in skillet. Stir well until brown. (Everything will be loosened from bottom of skillet.) Add 2½ to 3 cups water to mixture until it looks like gravy. Serve over cooked rice.

Meat Loaf with Sauce

MEAT LOAF:
2 pounds ground beef
½ cup oatmeal
½ cup soft bread crumbs
4 eggs
1 medium onion, diced
¼ cup dill pickle juice

SAUCE:
½ cup ketchup
¼ cup water
2 teaspoons sugar
1 teaspoon Worcestershire sauce
½ cup dill pickles, diced

Mix meat loaf ingredients thoroughly and shape loaf in greased pan.
Mix sauce ingredients and pour over shaped loaf. Bake at 350° for 1 to 1½ hours.

Mexican Casserole

1 pound hamburger
½ onion, chopped
1 can cream of chicken soup
8 ounces taco sauce
1 can enchilada sauce
Corn tortillas
Cheddar cheese, shredded
1 can sliced ripe black olives (optional)

Brown meat and onion; drain. Add soup and sauces. In 9 x 13-inch casserole dish, layer half of tortillas, half of meat mixture, and half of cheese; repeat. Top with olives if desired. Bake at 350° for 20 to 30 minutes.

Include the gift of one of your well-loved recipes with your Christmas cards this year. Choose holiday-themed recipe cards and write in festive-colored ink (or use your computer to save time). Write one of your favorite scriptures on the backs of the recipe cards. Your friends and family will be delighted with this thoughtful gift.

Mustard-Glazed Ham

1 (8 to 10 pound) ham, cooked
1 small jar apple jelly
1 small jar pineapple preserves
1 (1 ounce) container dry mustard
2 tablespoons prepared horseradish
Salt and black pepper to taste

Bake ham at 325° for 1 hour 45 minutes. Combine remaining ingredients and brush over ham. Return ham to oven for 35 to 45 minutes or until meat thermometer inserted in ham reads 140°.

Oven Beef Stew

1 pound beef stew meat, cut up
1 package onion soup mix
1 can beef broth
1 can cream of mushroom soup
1 soup can of water

Add desired amounts of the following:
Carrots, peeled and cut into chunks
Potatoes, peeled and cut into chunks
Onions, peeled and cut into chunks

Combine all ingredients. Cook for 3 hours in 300° oven or 4- or 6-quart roaster.

Use a colorful quilt for your holiday tablecloth.

Pecan-Chicken Casserole

2 cups cooked chicken, chopped
½ cup pecans, chopped
2 teaspoons minced onion
2 cups celery, chopped
1 cup mayonnaise
2 teaspoons lemon juice
1 cup potato chips, broken
½ cup cheddar cheese, shredded

Mix first six ingredients together. Place in greased 1½-quart casserole. Mix chips and cheese and sprinkle on top. Bake, uncovered, at 350° for 30 minutes.

Savory Pork Roast

1 (4 pound) boneless top loin pork roast
1 clove garlic, cut in half
1 teaspoon dried sage leaves
1 teaspoon dried marjoram leaves
1 teaspoon salt
Grapes (optional)

Using cut sides of garlic, rub pork roast. Mix sage, marjoram, and salt;
sprinkle on roast, then place meat fat side up in shallow roasting pan. Insert meat
thermometer in thickest part of pork and roast, uncovered, at 325° for 2 to 2½ hours
or until meat thermometer registers 170°. Garnish with frosted grapes (dipped
in water and rolled in sugar) if desired.

Shepherd's Pie

1½ pounds ground beef
1 medium onion, chopped
1 can tomato soup
1 (15 ounce) can tomato sauce
1 can whole kernel sweet corn
1 can cut green beans
Cheddar cheese, shredded
8 potatoes, cooked and sliced
Salt and garlic powder to taste
Cheese spread

Brown ground beef with onion; drain. Add next six ingredients. Season with salt and garlic powder. Pour into 9 x 13-inch baking dish. Top with cheese spread. Bake at 350° for approximately 40 minutes.

Spaghetti Sauce with Meatballs

SAUCE:
1 (family size) jar tomato sauce
2 small cans tomato paste
  (fill each can 3 times with water)
1 small onion, chopped
½ teaspoon garlic salt
½ teaspoon sugar
4 tablespoons cheese, shredded
½ teaspoon oregano
¼ teaspoon sweet basil
Salt and black pepper to taste

MEATBALLS:
1½ pounds hamburger
3 slices bread (soak in water then
  squeeze out the water)
½ onion, chopped
Garlic salt to taste
Salt and black pepper to taste

Combine sauce ingredients in large saucepan. Add meatballs to sauce
and cook over low heat for approximately 2 hours.

Spinach and Mushroom Chicken Alfredo

1 (10 ounce) package frozen
    creamed spinach
1 to 2 tablespoons cornstarch
1½ cups milk, divided
4 boneless, skinless chicken breasts
12 tablespoons olive oil
1 small jar or can sliced mushrooms, drained

1 to 2 cloves garlic
2 tablespoons butter
½ cup Parmesan cheese, grated
8 ounces spiral-shaped pasta,
    cooked

Prepare spinach according to package directions. Set aside. In small bowl, mix 1 tablespoon cornstarch with ½ cup milk to make paste. Set aside. Slice chicken into thin strips. Heat olive oil in large frying pan over medium-high heat. Add mushrooms, garlic, and chicken to pan. Stir-fry until chicken browns. Remove chicken-mushroom mixture to a separate plate and keep warm.

Alfredo sauce: In same frying pan, melt butter. Stir bowl of cornstarch paste. Add to melted butter along with Parmesan cheese and remaining milk. Cook and stir until thick.

Return chicken-mushroom mixture to pan. Add prepared spinach to pan. Heat and stir Alfredo until bubbly. Serve over hot, cooked spiral shaped pasta.

Traditional Christmas Turkey

1 (10 to 12 pound) whole turkey
6 tablespoons butter, cut into slices
4 cups warm water
3 cubes chicken bouillon
2 tablespoons parsley flakes
2 tablespoons minced onion
2 tablespoons seasoned salt
2 tablespoons poultry seasoning

Rinse and wash turkey. Remove neck and discard giblets. Place turkey in roasting pan. Separate skin from breast and place slices of butter between skin and breast meat. In medium bowl, dissolve bouillon in water. Stir in parsley and minced onion and pour mixture over top of turkey. Sprinkle turkey with seasoned salt and poultry seasoning. Cover with foil and bake at 350° for 3½ to 4 hours, until internal temperature of turkey reaches 180°. Remove foil during last 45 minutes to brown turkey.

Lord, remind me to give myself a "time-out" this month—so that I take a break from the tasks that keep me busy and longing for free time during the entire month of December. While there are several important items I must accomplish for the Christmas holiday, help me to pare down my list so that I don't get wrapped up in the things that don't matter much but that rob me of precious time. There's no better way to spend my time than with You and my family, Father. Amen.

Savory Sides

Faith is to believe, on the Word of God, what we do not see,
and its reward is to see and enjoy what we believe.
St. Augustine

Apple-Cabbage Coleslaw

½ large cabbage, shredded
1 red apple, cored and chopped with peel
½ cup fat-free salad dressing
1 pinch salt
½ tablespoon white vinegar
6 packages artificial sweetener
2 tablespoons skim milk

Place shredded cabbage and chopped apple in large bowl. Mix together salad dressing, salt, vinegar, artificial sweetener, and milk. Pour over cabbage and apple. Mix well. Chill before serving. Keeps several days in refrigerator.

Applesauce

2 large cooking apples, peeled, cored, and chopped
2 tablespoons apple juice
1 tablespoon butter
1 tablespoon light brown sugar
1 star anise seedpod
Salt and freshly ground black pepper

Place all ingredients except salt and pepper in pan; cook uncovered over medium heat for 15 minutes, stirring occasionally until fruit is soft. Remove star anise and puree fruit mixture in food processor. Season with salt and pepper.

Asparagus Casserole

4 slices bread, toasted
1 can asparagus, drained, juice reserved
1 can cream of chicken soup
Cheddar cheese, shredded

Break toasted bread in bottom of casserole dish. Put drained asparagus on top of bread. Mix asparagus juice with cream of chicken soup. Pour over mixture. Top with cheese. Bake at 400° for 45 minutes to 1 hour.

Baked Garden Vegetables

1 cup carrots, julienned
2 cups potatoes, peeled and sliced
1 package frozen baby lima beans
2 medium zucchini, quartered and sliced
2 cups bok choy, coarsely chopped (may use cabbage)
¼ cup butter (not margarine)
3 tablespoons fresh parsley, minced
¼ teaspoon salt-free seasoning
½ teaspoon sea salt
Freshly ground black pepper

Layer all vegetables in heavy casserole. Dot with butter; sprinkle with parsley
and seasonings. Cover casserole and bake at 325° for 45 to 60 minutes or until tender.
Toss with additional butter if desired. Serve with fresh diced tomatoes.
Serves 4 to 6.

Give a living gift of a homegrown houseplant or herbs you've cultivated from seeds. Take clippings from a hearty plant such as an ivy, philodendron, or spider plant. Start them in a tin, a clay pot, a coffee mug, an old boot, a lined basket, or any unique pot. Keep soil moist until rooted. Attach plant care instructions with a ribbon.

Barbecued Beans

1 pound hamburger
1 onion, chopped
4 (1 pound) cans pork and beans
1 tablespoon Worcestershire sauce
Salt and black pepper to taste
2 tablespoons vinegar
2 tablespoons brown sugar
½ cup ketchup
1 dash chili powder

Brown hamburger and onion in large skillet; drain off fat. Add remaining ingredients.
Transfer to casserole and bake at 350° for 35 minutes. Or leave in skillet, cooking over
low heat and stirring often, until boiling. Simmer for 10 to 15 minutes.

Broccoli and Rice Casserole

3 stalks fresh or 1 box frozen broccoli, steamed
1 cup short- or long-grain brown or white rice, cooked
1 can cream of chicken soup (or cream of celery or mushroom)
½ cup mayonnaise
3 cups cheddar, Colby, or other favorite cheese, shredded

Mix steamed broccoli, cooked rice, soup, mayonnaise, and 1 cup cheese together.
Add salt and black pepper to taste. Pour into casserole, and top with remaining cheese.
Bake at 375° for 20 to 30 minutes or until cheese on top is bubbly.

Brussels Sprouts and Chestnuts

2¼ pounds brussels sprouts
2 cups chicken broth
1 (8 ounce) can chestnuts
2 tablespoons butter
Salt (optional)
Freshly ground black pepper

Cut a slice from base of each brussels sprout and tear off outer leaves. Bring chicken stock to a boil in pan and place steamer containing sprouts over pan and cover. Steam for 6 to 8 minutes, until sprouts are tender.
Stir sprouts and chestnuts in melted butter over medium heat for 2 to 3 minutes. Transfer to warm serving dish and season with pepper. Serves 8.

*Christmas is the season of the "gimmes."
Instead of focusing on your wants this
Christmas, keep your thoughts centered
on the blessings the Lord has bestowed
upon you this year. Take time to praise
God for His goodness—and turn your
"gimmes" into "thanks."*

Give thanks to the Lord, for he is good.
Psalm 136:1

Carrot Soufflé

2 pounds cooked carrots
2 cups sugar
6 eggs
1 cup margarine
6 tablespoons flour
2 teaspoons baking powder
2 teaspoons vanilla

Blend or mash carrots; gradually add other ingredients, adding baking powder and vanilla last. Beat until smooth. Place in casserole. Bake at 350° for 30 to 45 minutes, until firm.

Corn Bread Stuffing

CORN BREAD:

1¼ cups flour
¾ cup cornmeal
¼ cup sugar
2 teaspoons baking powder

½ teaspoon salt
1 cup milk
¼ cup vegetable oil
2 eggs, beaten

In mixing bowl, blend together dry ingredients. Stir in milk, oil, and eggs. Pour into greased 8- or 9-inch square baking dish and bake at 400° for 20 to 25 minutes. Cool.

STUFFING:

1 pound fresh mushrooms, sliced
1 cup celery, chopped
¾ cup onion, chopped
½ cup butter

1⅔ cups water
4 chicken-flavored bouillon cubes
1 pound sausage, browned and drained
1½ teaspoons poultry seasoning

Sauté mushrooms, celery, and onion in butter until tender. Add water and bouillon cubes; cook until bouillon is completely dissolved. Set aside to cool. In large mixing bowl, crumble corn bread. Pour in mushroom mixture and remaining ingredients. Mix well. Bake at 350° for 30 to 40 minutes.

Corn Casserole

1 can sweet whole kernel corn, drained
2 eggs, lightly beaten
1 small box corn muffin mix
½ cup butter, melted
1 (8 ounce) container sour cream

Combine all ingredients. Place in greased 9 x 9-inch baking pan.
Bake at 350° for 45 to 50 minutes or until golden brown.

Corn Chowder

½ pound bacon
½ cup onion, chopped
½ cup celery, chopped
2 tablespoons flour
4 cups milk
⅛ teaspoon black pepper
2 cans cream-style corn
Fresh parsley, chopped
Paprika

In saucepan, fry bacon until crisp. Remove bacon from pan, crumble, and set aside.
Drain fat, reserving 3 tablespoons in saucepan. Cook onion and celery in bacon drippings
until tender; remove from heat. Stir in flour. Cook over medium heat, stirring constantly,
until mixture is bubbly; remove from heat. Stir in milk. Heat to boiling, stirring constantly.
Boil and stir for 1 minute. Reduce heat. Stir in pepper and corn.
Cook until soup is heated through. Remove from heat and ladle into soup bowls.
Garnish with cooked bacon and a sprinkling of parsley and paprika.

Cream of Pumpkin Soup

1 cup onion, chopped
2 tablespoons butter, melted
2 (14.5 ounce) cans chicken broth
1 (15 ounce) can pumpkin
1 teaspoon salt
¼ teaspoon ground cinnamon
⅛ teaspoon ground ginger
⅛ teaspoon black pepper
1 cup half-and-half

In medium saucepan, sauté onion in butter until tender. Slowly add 1 can chicken broth; stir well. Bring to a boil; cover, reduce heat, and simmer for 15 minutes. Transfer broth mixture into blender or food processor. Process until smooth. Return processed mixture to saucepan. Stir in remaining can of broth, pumpkin, and spices. Bring to a boil; cover, reduce heat, and simmer for 10 minutes, stirring occasionally.
Stir in half-and-half and heat through. Do not boil. Garnish as desired.

Creamy Corn

1 (20 ounce) package frozen corn
1 (8 ounce) package cream cheese, softened
½ cup butter
3 teaspoons sugar
6 tablespoons water

Place corn, cream cheese, butter, sugar, and water in slow cooker.
Cook on low for 4 to 5 hours.

Fresh Broccoli Salad

1 package fresh broccoli
3 stalks celery (or 1 large Vidalia onion)
1 cup raisins
½ cup bacon bits (or 6 slices cooked, crumbled bacon)
1 tablespoon vinegar
1 teaspoon sugar
3 tablespoons mayonnaise

Chop florets of broccoli and celery (or onion). Add other ingredients.
Mix with mayonnaise. Chill for 1 hour or longer.

Fresh Cranberry Salad

2 cups water
¾ cup sugar
3 cups (12 ounces) fresh cranberries
1 (6 ounce) package orange-flavored gelatin
1 (8.25 ounce) can crushed pineapple
½ cup celery or walnuts, chopped
Salad greens

Place water and sugar in 2-quart saucepan and bring to a boil; boil for 1 minute.
Add cranberries and return to a boil for 5 minutes. Add gelatin and stir until dissolved.
Stir in pineapple (including liquid) and celery or walnuts. Pour into 6-cup mold and
chill at least 6 hours, until firm. Unmold onto salad greens.
Garnish with pineapple chunks and sour cream if desired.

Old coffee cans make great gift containers. Paint the outside of the can. Add a design with paint or permanent markers. You can also use stickers or glue on foam shapes, sequins, and ribbons. Decorate the lid with a piece of fabric.

Golden Squash Casserole

6 cups cubed, pared Hubbard squash*
1 cup sour cream
2 tablespoons margarine or butter
1 medium onion, finely chopped
1 teaspoon salt
¼ teaspoon black pepper

Place 1 inch of salted water in pan and bring to a boil. Add squash, cover, and return to a boil. Cook for 15 to 20 minutes or until tender; drain. After mashing squash, stir in remaining ingredients. Pour into ungreased 1-quart casserole. Bake, uncovered, at 325° for 35 to 45 minutes or until hot.

Note: 2 packages (12 ounces each) frozen cooked squash, thawed, can be substituted for the fresh squash.

Green Bean Casserole

2 quarts green beans, drained
2 cans cream of mushroom soup
Salt and black pepper to taste
Milk
1 large can French fried onion rings

Mix beans, soup, and salt and pepper with enough milk to slightly dilute soup.
Spread in cake pan and sprinkle with onion rings. Bake at 350° until bubbly
and onion rings are slightly brown.

Green Peas with Celery and Onion

2 packages (10 ounces each) frozen peas
½ cup celery, sliced
1 small onion, thinly sliced
3 tablespoons margarine or butter, softened
¼ teaspoon salt

Following directions on package for peas, cook celery, onion, and peas; drain.
Stir in margarine and salt.

Use three-ring binders to create family cookbooks to give as gifts at your Christmas get-together. Include recipes for all the family favorites with a brief bio and photo of the creator of each dish. These will be cherished for years to come.

Hash Brown Potato Casserole

1 (2 pound) bag frozen hash browns
½ cup margarine or butter, melted
½ to 1 teaspoon salt
½ teaspoon black pepper
1 can cream of chicken soup (regular or reduced fat/sodium)
1 pint sour cream (regular or low-fat)
¼ cup onion, chopped
8 to 10 ounces cheddar cheese, shredded
2 cups ham, cooked and diced (optional)
1 cup cornflakes
3 tablespoons butter, melted

Mix all ingredients except cornflakes and melted butter. Pour in large baking dish.
Sprinkle top with cornflakes and butter. Bake at 350° for 1½ hours.

VARIATION:
Add 1 can cream of potato soup (regular or reduced fat/low-sodium)
in place of the cream of chicken soup.

Layered Salad

1 head lettuce, shredded
2 cucumbers, diced
2 tomatoes, diced
1 medium onion, diced
6 radishes, thinly sliced
1 medium bell pepper, diced
1 pound bacon, cooked and crumbled
Salt and black pepper to taste
1 (3 ounce) can English peas, drained
1 (3 ounce) can sweet whole kernel corn, drained
2 cups mayonnaise
1 pound cheddar cheese, shredded

Arrange salad ingredients in large casserole or oblong pan, one at a time, layering as you go. Spread mayonnaise over salad ingredients and sprinkle cheddar cheese on top. Serve using an egg turner.

Mixed Vegetable Medley

1 (10 ounce) package frozen peas
1 (10 ounce) package frozen green beans
1 (10 ounce) package frozen cauliflower
¾ cup water
1 (2 ounce) jar sliced pimiento, drained
2 tablespoons margarine or butter
½ teaspoon dried basil leaves
½ teaspoon salt
⅛ teaspoon black pepper

Bring vegetables and water to a boil and reduce heat. Cover and cook over low heat about 7 minutes or until vegetables are tender. Drain, then stir in remaining ingredients.

Make an edible wreath. Create a ring of green grape bunches on a plate. Add a few accents of red grapes or cherries. Add a red bow to the plate.

Party Potatoes

10 to 12 medium potatoes, cooked and mashed
1 (8 ounce) package cream cheese, softened
1 cup sour cream
2 tablespoons chives, chopped
1 cup cheddar cheese, shredded
Salt and black pepper to taste
2 tablespoons butter

Beat together first six ingredients. Place in greased 9 x 13-inch baking dish.
Cover and refrigerate until 1 hour before serving time. Preheat oven to 350°.
Dot potatoes with butter. Bake for 1 hour or until potatoes reach desired tenderness.

Pecan Sweet Potatoes

6 medium sweet potatoes, baked, cooled, and peeled
½ cup brown sugar
½ cup pecans, chopped
1 tablespoon orange peel
1 cup orange juice
1½ tablespoons butter, cut up
½ teaspoon salt

Lightly spray 9 x 13-inch baking pan with vegetable spray. Slice potatoes in ¼-inch slices,
layer in pan and set aside. In small bowl, combine brown sugar, pecans, and orange peel.
Pour mixture over sweet potatoes. Pour orange juice over all. Dot with butter.
Season with salt to taste. Cover and refrigerate until ready to use.
Bake at 350° for 45 minutes; uncover and cook 15 to 20 minutes longer.

Roasted Potato Bites

12 to 15 small red potatoes
1 cup cheddar cheese, shredded
½ cup real or light mayonnaise
½ cup green onion, minced
½ pound bacon, cooked and crumbled
2 tablespoons fresh basil, chopped

Bake potatoes until tender. Allow to cool enough to handle. Cut crosswise in half. Cut a thin slice from bottom so they stand upright. Scoop out potatoes leaving ¼ inch rim in shell. Combine scooped potatoes with rest of ingredients. Spoon into potato shells. Bake at 375° for 3 to 5 minutes or until brown. Serve hot.

Roman Pasta Salad

1 pound thin spaghetti (or other shaped pasta)
2 large tomatoes
1 large onion
1 large cucumber
1 large green pepper
16 ounces Italian dressing
1 envelope Italian dressing mix

Cook and cool pasta; set aside. Dice vegetables. Mix vegetables
with Italian dressing and mix. Add to cool pasta; refrigerate overnight.

Squash Dressing

1 cup diced onion
½ cup margarine
2 cups corn bread
2 cups yellow squash, cooked and mashed
2 cups diced chicken
Salt and black pepper to taste
1 can cream of chicken soup
1 can sliced mushrooms
1 teaspoon ground sage
2 eggs, beaten

Sauté onion in margarine. Mix all ingredients in casserole and
bake at 350° for 30 to 40 minutes, until brown on top.

Sweet Potato Casserole

CASSEROLE:
3 cups mashed sweet potatoes
¼ cup butter or margarine, melted
1⅓ cups sugar
½ teaspoon salt
2 eggs
½ cup milk
1 teaspoon vanilla

TOPPING:
1⅓ cups brown sugar
⅓ cup flour
½ cup flaked coconut
¼ cup butter or margarine, softened
½ cup pecans, chopped

Mix sweet potatoes with remaining casserole ingredients. Pour into greased
9 x 13-inch baking dish. Mix topping ingredients together and spread evenly
over sweet potato mixture. Bake at 325° for 35 to 40 minutes.

Taco Salad

1 pound ground beef, browned and drained
1 package taco seasoning
1 small head lettuce, shredded
1 medium onion, diced
1 green pepper, diced
3 small tomatoes, chopped
1 cup cheddar cheese, shredded
1 can kidney beans
1 (14 ounce) package tortilla chips, broken
1 bottle ranch dressing with bacon

Mix taco seasoning into ground beef. Cool in refrigerator. Just before serving,
mix in remaining ingredients and toss with dressing.

Tangy Ranch Green Beans

2 tablespoons butter or margarine
2 packages frozen French-cut green beans, partially thawed
1 can sliced mushrooms, drained
1 envelope package ranch dressing mix
3 to 4 slices bacon, cooked and crumbled

In skillet, melt butter. Stir in green beans and cook until tender. Mix in mushrooms and ranch dressing mix. Heat through. Before serving, sprinkle crumbled bacon over beans.

Wild Rice Stuffing

½ cup wild rice
2½ cups water
½ cup brown rice
2 chicken-flavored bouillon cubes
¼ teaspoon ground sage
½ teaspoon salt
½ teaspoon black pepper
3 cups fresh mushrooms, sliced
1 cup celery, chopped
1 small sweet onion, chopped
½ cup slivered almonds, toasted (optional)

In large saucepan, combine wild rice, water, brown rice, bouillon cubes, sage, salt, and pepper. Bring to a boil; reduce heat. Cover and simmer for 20 minutes. Stir in mushrooms, celery, and onion. Cook covered over medium-low heat for 25 minutes or until vegetables are just tender, stirring frequently. Garnish with toasted almonds if desired.

Decadent Desserts

Faith is not a sense, nor sight, nor reason,
but simply taking God at His word.
CHRISTMAS EVANS

Black Forest Cake

2 (20 ounce) cans tart pitted cherries,
  undrained
1 cup sugar
¼ cup cornstarch
1½ teaspoons vanilla extract

2 (9 inch) chocolate cake layers, baked
  and cooled
3 cups cold whipping cream
⅓ cup powdered sugar

Drain cherries, reserving ½ cup juice. Combine reserved cherry juice, cherries, sugar, and cornstarch in saucepan. Cook and stir over low heat until thickened. Add vanilla; stir. Divide each cake layer in half horizontally. Crumble one half layer; set aside. Beat cold whipping cream and powdered sugar in large bowl with electric mixer on high until stiff peaks form. Reserve 1½ cups whipped cream for decorative piping. Place one cake layer on serving plate. Spread with 1 cup whipped cream; top with ¾ cup cherry topping. Top with second cake layer, 1 cup whipped cream, and ¾ cup cherry topping; top with third cake layer. Frost cake sides with remaining whipped cream; pat gently with reserved cake crumbs. Spoon reserved 1½ cups whipped cream into pastry bag fitted with star tip; pipearound top and bottom edges of cake. Spoon remaining topping over top of cake.

Bûche de Noël
(Yule Log Cake)

CAKE:

1 cup flour
1¼ teaspoons baking powder
¼ teaspoon salt
1 tablespoon cocoa
4 eggs
⅔ cup sugar
1 tablespoon hot water

FILLING:

½ cup butter or margarine, softened
2¼ cups powdered sugar
2 tablespoons cocoa
2 to 3 tablespoons milk

Sift together flour, baking powder, salt, and cocoa. In bowl over pan of hot water, whisk together eggs and sugar until pale and thick. Remove from heat and fold in half the flour mixture. Fold in remaining flour mixture, along with hot water. Pour batter into lined jelly-roll pan. Bake at 425° for about 10 minutes. Turn cake onto sheet of waxed paper and trim edges of cake. Before it cools, roll up cake with paper inside. Set aside to cool. For filling, mix butter and powdered sugar. Beat in cocoa and milk until mixture is fluffy. Unroll cake and remove paper. Spread one-quarter of filling on cake and roll it up. Spread rest of filling on outside of log. Use fork to make swirls and ridges like tree bark.
Decorate with powdered sugar if desired.

You've created a wonderful culinary treat; now share it with your family and friends with a little flare. Create a bag to carry, as well as show off, your treat. Cut a holiday design into the side of a sturdy paper bag. Cover the inside with clear or colored plastic wrap. Fill and let a hint of the contents show through, then fold the top over. With a hole punch, make two holes at least an inch apart. Pull ribbon, raffia, or yarn through the holes and tie a bow that hangs above the window.

Christmas Cake in a Snap

1 box white cake mix
Red and green food coloring

Prepare cake as directed. Divide batter into two bowls. Add red food coloring to one part and green food coloring to the other. Bake in two layer pans. When cakes are cool, slice each cakes in half lengthwise. Whip up your favorite white icing. Alternate colored layers with icing. Decorate cake with candy and sprinkles.

Creamy Baked Cheesecake

¼ cup butter or margarine, melted
1 cup graham cracker crumbs
¼ cup sugar
2 (8 ounce) packages cream cheese, softened
1 (14 ounce) can sweetened condensed milk
3 eggs
¼ teaspoon salt
¼ cup lemon juice
Fruit topping, optional

In small bowl, combine butter, cracker crumbs, and sugar. Press into bottom of buttered 9-inch springform pan. In large mixing bowl, beat cream cheese until fluffy. Add sweetened condensed milk, eggs, and salt. Beat well. Stir in lemon juice. Pour batter over cracker crust. Bake at 300° for 50 to 55 minutes or until cheesecake springs back when lightly touched. Cool completely, then chill. Serve with fruit topping of your choice.

Easy Chocolate Fudge

1 cup granulated sugar
¼ cup cocoa
⅓ cup milk
¼ cup margarine or butter
1 tablespoon light corn syrup
1 teaspoon vanilla
⅓ cup nuts, chopped
2 to 2¼ cups powdered sugar

Combine granulated sugar and cocoa in 2-quart saucepan. Stir in milk, margarine, and corn syrup. Bring to a boil over medium heat, stirring frequently. Boil and stir for 1 minute. Remove from heat and allow to cool without stirring until bottom of pan is lukewarm (about 45 minutes). Stir in vanilla and nuts. Mix in powdered sugar until very stiff. Press in buttered loaf pan measuring 9 x 5 x 3 inches. Chill until firm and cut into 1-inch squares.

German Chocolate Cake

2 cups flour	1 cup water
2 cups sugar	2 eggs
½ teaspoon salt	1 teaspoon baking soda
1 cup butter	½ cup buttermilk
3 tablespoons cocoa	1 teaspoon vanilla

Sift together twice flour, sugar, and salt. In saucepan, place butter, cocoa, and water. Bring to a boil; stir until butter is melted. Beat cocoa mixture slowly into flour mixture. Beat together eggs, baking soda, buttermilk, and vanilla. Add to other mixture and mix well. Bake in greased 10 x 13-inch pan at 350° for 30 to 45 minutes.

FROSTING:

1 cup canned cream	1 teaspoon vanilla
1 cup sugar	1 cup coconut
3 egg yolks	1 cup pecans
½ cup margarine	

Combine first five ingredients in saucepan. Cook, stirring, over medium heat for 12 minutes or until mixture thickens. Remove from heat. Add coconut and pecans. Beat until cool. Spread on cake in pan.

Gingerbread

2 cups flour
1½ teaspoons baking soda
2½ teaspoons ground ginger
½ teaspoon allspice
¼ teaspoon salt
⅔ cup molasses
⅔ cup sour cream
½ cup butter, softened
½ cup brown sugar
2 eggs, lightly beaten

Grease and flour 9-inch square baking pan. In small bowl, mix together flour, baking soda, ginger, allspice, and salt. In another small bowl, mix together molasses and sour cream. In large mixing bowl, cream butter and brown sugar. Add eggs and beat well. Alternating between wet and dry ingredients, gradually add flour and molasses mixtures. Beat well after each addition. Pour batter into prepared pan. Bake at 350° for 30 to 35 minutes or until cake pulls away from sides of pan and toothpick comes out clean.

Kentucky Derby Pie

4 eggs, beaten
½ cup butter, melted
¾ cup brown sugar
1 cup light corn syrup
1 cup chocolate chips
1 cup pecans, chopped
1 teaspoon vanilla
1 teaspoon flour
1 unbaked pie shell

Mix all ingredients and pour into pie shell. Bake at 350° for 40 to 45 minutes.

Dear Heavenly Father, please offer peace to the hearts of families as they struggle through the hustle and bustle of the holiday season. We are in such a rush to accomplish our everyday tasks—and now with the Christmas holiday in our midst, the days are much more hectic. Remind us all of the importance of family and of the awesome meaning of Christmas— Your sending us the gift of Your Son. Help us to slow down and to take a moment to reflect on Your love daily.

*I heard the bells on Christmas Day
Their old familiar carols play,
And wild and sweet the words repeat
Of peace on earth, good will to men!*
HENRY WADSWORTH LONGFELLOW

Magic Cookie Bars

½ cup margarine or butter
1½ cups graham cracker crumbs
1 (14 ounce) can sweetened condensed milk
1 (6 ounce) package semisweet chocolate chips
1⅓ cups flaked coconut
1 cup nuts, chopped

In 9 x 13-inch baking pan, melt margarine in oven. Sprinkle crumbs over margarine, mix together, and press into pan. Pour sweetened condensed milk evenly over crumbs. Top evenly with remaining ingredients. Press down firmly. Bake at 350° (or 325° for glass dish) for 25 to 30 minutes or until lightly browned. Cool thoroughly before cutting.

Miniature Cheesecakes

2 eggs
2 (8 ounce) packages cream cheese, softened
½ cup sugar
1 teaspoon vanilla
1 can cherry pie filling

Beat first four ingredients until smooth. Line miniature muffin pans with paper liners. Fill each cup three quarters full with mixture. Bake at 350⁰ for 15 minutes. When cool, top each with one cherry from can of cherry pie filling. Makes approximately 48 cheesecakes.

Oatmeal Chocolate Chip Cake

1¾ cups boiling water
1 cup oats, quick or old fashioned
1 cup brown sugar
1 cup sugar
½ cup margarine
2 eggs (3 if small)

1¾ cups flour
1 teaspoon baking soda
½ teaspoon salt
1 tablespoon cocoa
1 cup chocolate chips
¾ cup walnuts, chopped

Pour boiling water over oats; let stand at room temperature for 10 minutes. Add both sugars and margarine to oatmeal. Stir with spoon until margarine melts. Add eggs and mix well. Add flour, baking soda, salt, and cocoa, stirring until well blended. Add half of chocolate chips. Pour batter into greased 9 x 13-inch pan. Sprinkle chopped nuts and rest of chocolate chips on top. Bake at 350° for 40 minutes. Needs no other frosting.

Pán de Pascua
(Christmas Cake)

1 cup butter or margarine, softened
1½ tablespoons warm water
2 cups powdered sugar
6 eggs, separated
1 cup seedless raisins
1⅓ cups mixed crystallized fruits, chopped
½ cup walnuts, broken

4¾ cups flour
2 tablespoons baking powder
1 teaspoon ground cinnamon
¼ teaspoon ground nutmeg
2 to 3 whole cloves
2 tablespoons rum flavoring
1 tablespoon vinegar
1 cup milk

Beat butter and warm water until fluffy. Add powdered sugar a little at a time. Beat in egg yolks. Mix in raisins, candied fruits, and walnuts by hand. Stir in flour, baking powder, spices, rum flavoring, and vinegar. Beat egg whites until soft peaks form, then fold into batter. Add enough milk so that batter drops from a spoon but is not too soft. Pour batter into greased and lined 8-inch round pan. Bake at 375° for 15 minutes. Reduce oven temperature to 325° and bake for 50 to 55 minutes. Cool for 10 minutes, then remove cake from pan to cool. Sprinkle with powdered sugar before serving.

Peanut Butter Pie

1 (8 ounce) package cream cheese, softened
1 cup powdered sugar
1 cup peanut butter
12 ounces whipped topping
1 graham cracker crust

Mix all ingredients, reserving small amount of whipped topping for topping if desired.
Pour into graham cracker crust. Refrigerate until ready to serve.

Pecan Pie

1 pastry shell, unbaked
1 cup pecans, chopped
3 eggs
½ cup sugar
1 cup light corn syrup
⅛ teaspoon salt
1 teaspoon vanilla
¼ cup butter, melted

Line pie plate with pastry. Spread pecans on top. Set aside. Beat eggs; add sugar,
corn syrup, salt, vanilla, and melted butter. Pour over top of pecans.
Bake at 350° for 50 to 60 minutes.

Peppermint Stick Cake

2⅔ cups flour
3 teaspoons baking powder
1 teaspoon salt
½ cup shortening
1½ cups sugar, divided
1¼ cups milk, divided
1 egg yolk, separated

1 teaspoon vanilla
½ cup peppermint stick candy,
  finely ground
½ cup peppermint stick candy,
  coarsely ground

Sift flour and measure. Sift again with baking powder and salt. Cream shortening. Continue creaming while gradually adding 1 cup sugar and 3 tablespoons milk. Add egg yolk and vanilla to remaining milk. Add sifted dry ingredients alternately with milk to creamed mixture. In separate bowl, beat egg white until stiff but not dry. Beat in remaining sugar. Fold in cake batter. Pour into two 9-inch pans or one 9 x 13-inch pan and sprinkle with finely ground candy. Bake at 350° for 25 minutes. Ice with white icing when cooled and sprinkle with coarsely ground candy.

Pineapple-Coconut Carrot Cake

1 cup vegetable oil
1½ to 2 cups sugar
3 eggs (4 if small)
2 cups flour
2 teaspoons baking soda
½ teaspoon salt
2 teaspoons ground cinnamon

1 cup crushed pineapple, drained
2 cups carrots, shredded
1 cup flaked coconut
1 cup nuts, chopped
1 teaspoon vanilla
1 cup raisins (optional)

Mix oil, sugar, and eggs. Add remaining ingredients.
Pour into lightly greased 9 x 13-inch pan and bake at 350° for 50 minutes.

FROSTING:

½ cup butter or margarine, softened
1 (8 ounce) package cream cheese, softened

2 cups powdered sugar
2 teaspoons vanilla
1 cup nuts, chopped

Cream first four ingredients with electric mixer. Fold in nuts. Spread on cooled cake.

Red Velvet Cake

½ cup shortening
1½ cups sugar
2 eggs
2 tablespoons cocoa
1½ ounces red food coloring
1 teaspoon salt

2½ cups flour
1 teaspoon vanilla
1 cup buttermilk
1 teaspoon baking soda
1 tablespoon vinegar

Cream shortening; add sugar gradually. Add eggs, one at a time; beat well. Make paste of cocoa and coloring; add to creamed mixture. Add salt, flour, and vanilla alternately with buttermilk, beating well after each addition. Sprinkle soda over vinegar; add to batter. Stir until thoroughly mixed. Bake in three 8-inch square pans or two 9-inch square pans at 350° for 30 minutes.

FROSTING:

2 (3 ounce) packages cream
  cheese, softened
6 tablespoons butter, softened

1 teaspoon vanilla
2 cups powdered sugar, sifted

Blend all ingredients until smooth. Spread on cooled cake.

138

Sugar Plums

4 ounces whole blanched almonds
1 (24 ounce) container pitted prunes
1 cup (4 ounces) flaked coconut
¼ cup sugar

Insert almond into each prune, molding fruit around nut to create plum shape. Mix coconut and sugar in small bowl and roll stuffed prunes in mixture. Store in airtight container with waxed paper between layers. Yields about 100.

Swedish Apple Pie

Enough apples, peeled cored, and sliced, to fill pie pan two-thirds full
1 tablespoon sugar
1 teaspoon ground cinnamon
¾ cup butter, melted
1 cup sugar
1 cup flour
1 egg
½ cup nuts
1 pinch salt

Fill pie pan ⅔ full with apples. Combine 1 tablespoon sugar with cinnamon; sprinkle over apples. In small bowl, combine butter, 1 cup sugar, flour, egg, nuts, and salt; mix thoroughly and spoon over apples. Bake at 350° for 35 minutes or until golden brown.

Toffee Bar Cake

1 box German chocolate cake mix
1 can sweetened condensed milk
1 jar caramel ice cream topping
1 (8 ounce) container whipped topping
3 to 6 chocolate toffee candy bars, crushed

Bake cake according to package directions. While cake is still hot, poke holes in cake about 1 inch apart, using handle of wooden spoon. Pour sweetened condensed milk and ice cream topping mixture over cake, making sure cake is completely covered. Refrigerate overnight. Before serving, garnish with whipped topping and sprinkle with toffee candy bar crumbs.

Note: Candy bars can be easily crushed by freezing them first, then breaking them with a hammer.

Traditional Pumpkin Pie

1 (15 ounce) can pumpkin
1 (14 ounce) can sweetened condensed milk
2 eggs, lightly beaten
1 teaspoon ground cinnamon
½ teaspoon ground ginger
½ teaspoon ground nutmeg
¼ teaspoon ground cloves
½ teaspoon salt
1 (9 inch) unbaked pie shell

Whisk pumpkin, sweetened condensed milk, eggs, spices, and salt in medium bowl until smooth. Pour into unbaked shell. Bake at 425° for 15 minutes, then reduce oven temperature to 350° and continue baking for 35 to 40 minutes or until knife inserted 1 inch from edge comes out clean. Cool.

Begin a new Christmas tradition with your family this year. Some ideas Martha and I love include the following:

- *Extend an invitation to your family members for a night of Christmas caroling. Gather at your house afterward for cookies and hot chocolate.*
- *Have a family photo taken and make your own Christmas cards. Personalize them with a special holiday message.*
- *Write a family Christmas letter to mail with your Christmas cards. Include important items such as job changes, a move, kids' ages and schooling, exciting family events and news, and anything else that might be of interest. Be sure to get the entire family involved in the writing!*
- *Have your family pick a "charity of the year" and make a special donation at Christmastime.*
- *Create delicious meals and desserts with your family and deliver them to families in need.*

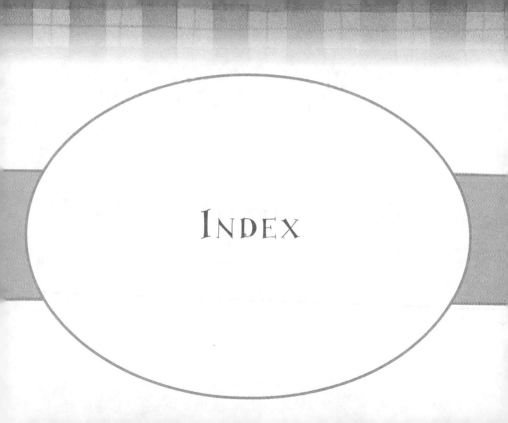

INDEX

BEST BEVERAGES

ABSOLUTELY AMAZING APPETIZERS

Mouthwatering Main Dishes

SAVORY SIDES

DECADENT DESSERTS

Also Available from Mary & Martha. . .

*In the Kitchen with
Mary & Martha*
ISBN 1-59310-878-8

One-Dish Wonders
ISBN 1-59789-011-1

Cookin' Up Christmas
ISBN 1-59789-239-4

224 pages • hardback with printed comb binding

Available Wherever Books Are Sold